WITHDRAWN

NARRATIVE

BLAZERS

CRIME SOLVERS

COMPUTER EVIDENCE

by Amy Kortuem

CAPSTONE PRESS
a capstone imprint

Blazers Books are published by Capstone Press,
1710 Roe Crest Drive, North Mankato, Minnesota 56003
www.mycapstone.com

Copyright © 2019 by Capstone Press, a Capstone imprint. All rights reserved.
No part of this publication may be reproduced in whole or in part, or stored
in a retrieval system, or transmitted in any form or by any means, electronic,
mechanical, photocopying, recording, or otherwise, without written
permission of the publisher.

Library of Congress Cataloging-in-Publication Data
Names: Kortuem, Amy, author.
Title: Computer evidence / by Amy Kortuem.
Description: North Mankato, Minnesota : Capstone Press, [2019] | Series:
   Blazers. Crime solvers. | Includes index.
Identifiers: LCCN 2018001963 (print) | LCCN 2018004524 (ebook) | ISBN
   9781543529982 (eBook PDF) | ISBN 9781543529906 (hardcover) | ISBN
   9781543529944 (pbk.)
Subjects: LCSH: Computer crimes—Investigation—Juvenile literature.
Classification: LCC HV8079.C65 (ebook) | LCC HV8079.C65 K67 2019 (print) |
   DDC 363.25/968—dc23
LC record available at https://lccn.loc.gov/2018001963

Editorial Credits
Carrie Braulick Sheely, editor; Kayla Rossow, designer; Svetlana Zhurkin,
media researcher; Kris Wilfahrt, production specialist

Photo Credits
Alamy: keith morris, 19; Courtesy of the Federal Bureau of Investigations, 7, 22,
29; Getty Images: AFP/Jay Directo, 23 (top), Pool/Gary W. Green, 27; Newscom:
Science Photo Library/Tek Image, 20, Zuma Press/Jebb Harris, 23 (bottom),
25; Shutterstock: Alexander Geiger, 16, Bing Wen, 28, charnsitr, 15, Eviart, 12,
Farosofa, 13, Gorodenkoff, 9 (top), igorstevanovic, 21, ioat, 9 (bottom), kaprik, 14,
Presslab, 18, rawf8, 5, Rawpixel, 10, Redpixel.pl, cover, 17

Design Elements by Shutterstock

Printed in the United States.
082018   000042

TABLE OF CONTENTS

Chapter 1
Clues Left on a Computer. 4

Chapter 2
Types of Computer Crimes. 8

Chapter 3
Finding and Gathering Computer Evidence 18

Chapter 4
Computer Evidence at Work. 26

Glossary 30
Read More 31
Internet Sites 31
Critical Thinking Questions 32
Index 32

Clues Left on a Computer

A worker opens an email and clicks on a link. A computer **virus** spreads. It shuts down all the company's computers. The company's owner calls the police.

virus—a hidden computer program that copies itself and harms computers

Police study the email. It traces back to a computer. Clues left on the computer show a former company worker likely made the virus. Computer **evidence** helps solve the crime.

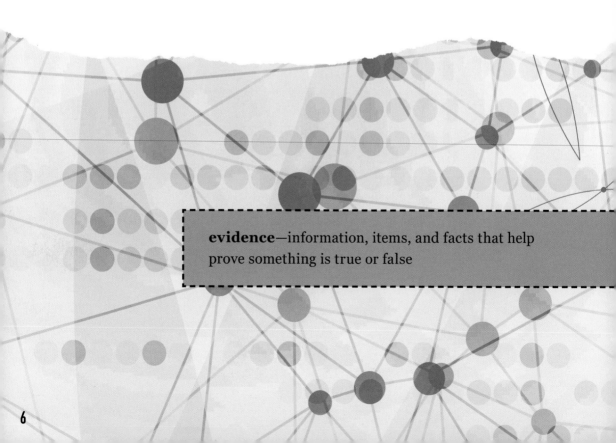

evidence—information, items, and facts that help prove something is true or false

Federal Bureau of Investigation (FBI) workers sometimes help local police solve computer crimes.

CHAPTER 2

Types of Computer Crimes

Criminals commit more than 1.5 million **cybercrimes** each year. Some criminals want to steal money or get information. **Hackers** may only want to damage computer systems.

> **criminal**—someone who commits a crime
>
> **cybercrime**—a crime that involves the Internet, a computer system, or computer technology
>
> **hacker**—a person who looks for ways to break into computer systems

❮ Hackers may work together to plan attacks.

FACT
Just one cybercrime can affect computers all over the world.

program—a series of step-by-step instructions that tells a computer what to do

Criminals may attach viruses to other **programs** or emails. A virus starts when someone opens the program or email attachment. The virus can then copy itself and damage other computers.

FACT

Sometimes companies hire hackers. The hackers find weaknesses in the companies' computer systems. The companies then can strengthen the systems to prevent attacks.

Some criminals use viruses to shut down computers or to steal **data**. They may ask for money before they will restart the computers or give information back. These viruses are called ransomware.

FACT

In May 2017 the ransomware WannaCry spread quickly. It shut down computers at companies in at least 150 countries.

data—information or facts

Pirates use or copy materials illegally. They often copy music, movies, and **software**. They may try to sell their illegal copies.

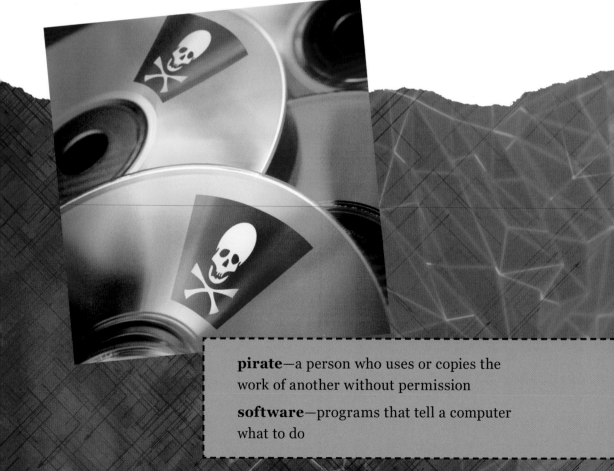

pirate—a person who uses or copies the work of another without permission

software—programs that tell a computer what to do

Some criminals **phish**. They may send an email with an attachment. The message tricks people into opening it. Then a program lets the criminal get information or steal money.

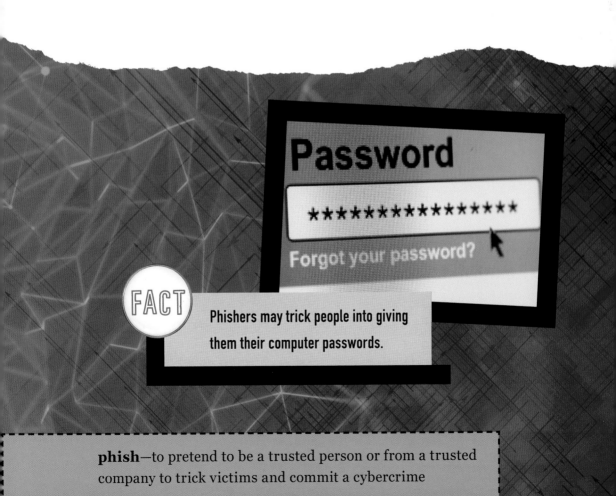

Password

****

Forgot your password?

FACT

Phishers may trick people into giving them their computer passwords.

phish—to pretend to be a trusted person or from a trusted company to trick victims and commit a cybercrime

CHAPTER 3

Finding and Gathering Computer Evidence

^ a cell phone found at a crime scene

Police and Federal Bureau of Investigation (FBI) workers solve computer crimes. They search crime **scenes** for computer evidence. They look for computers, cell phones, and other **digital devices**.

⌃ A crime scene investigator (CSI) checks a computer for clues at a crime scene.

scene—the place of an event or action

digital—involving a computer or other electronics

device—a piece of equipment that does a particular job

A CSI wraps a keyboard in a bag to protect evidence.

Police handle devices carefully. They wear gloves. The gloves protect any fingerprints on the items. Fingerprints can help show who has used a device. Police place the devices in bags.

FACT

Police often take pictures of devices before moving them.
The photos show where the devices were found.

Police take the devices to a crime lab. They search the devices for evidence. They use programs to search computer **hard drives**. Police can even find information that has been deleted.

hard drive—a device for storing computer data

The hacker group Anonymous is made up of people all over the world. They claim to hack for causes they support, such as free speech.

❮ Masked Anonymous members take part in a rally in Manila, Philippines.

⌄ An investigator shows a system that allows another hard drive to be read at a lab.

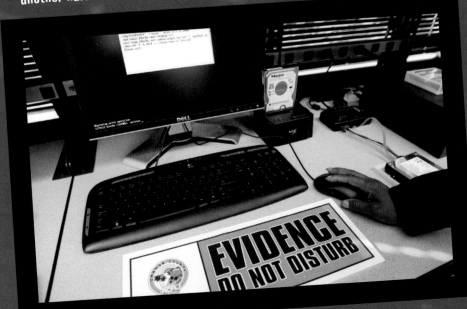

Police may put a tracking device inside a computer keyboard. They return the computer to the **suspect**. The device records what is typed. Police may also put **spyware** on a computer. It tracks websites visited.

suspect—someone thought to be responsible for a crime

spyware—software that is installed secretly and gathers information about a computer user's Internet use and personal data

FACT

Police may investigate cyberbullying. This type of bullying takes place through computers, cell phones, and other devices.

An investigator holds a device that can track what is typed on a keyboard.

CHAPTER 4

Computer Evidence at Work

Police might talk about computer evidence in court. They might show what they found. They also may explain how they found the evidence. It can help show that someone is **guilty**.

⌃ A CSI shows a cell phone in court
that was collected as evidence.

guilty—found to be responsible for a crime

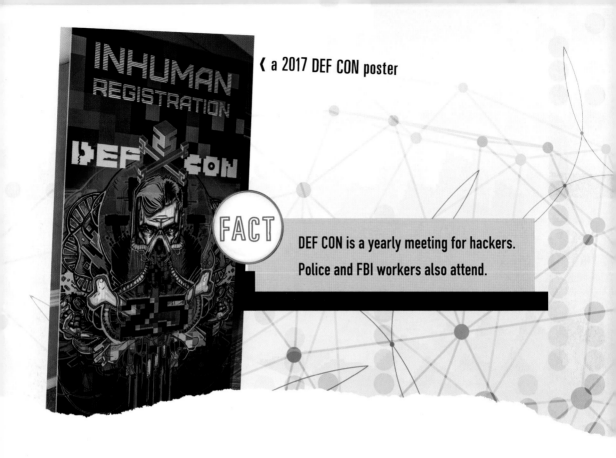

a 2017 DEF CON poster

FACT

DEF CON is a yearly meeting for hackers.
Police and FBI workers also attend.

Computer crimes can be hard
to solve. People keep finding new
ways to commit these crimes. Police
also need to find new ways to get
evidence and protect computers.

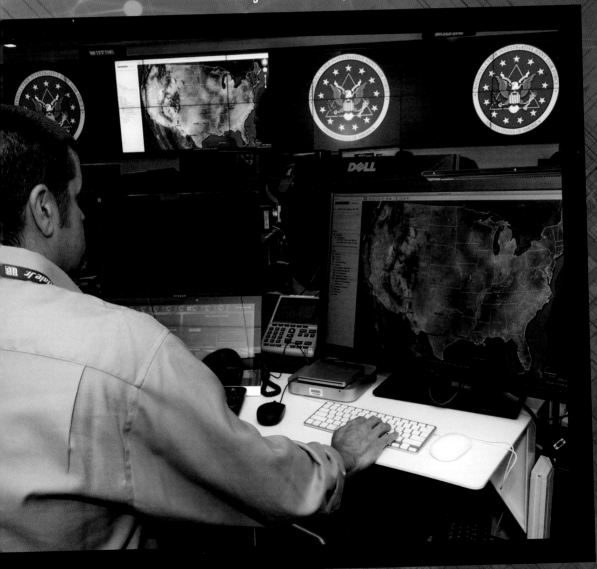

FBI workers and other team members work to protect U.S. government computers from cyberattacks.

GLOSSARY

criminal (KRI-muh-nuhl)—someone who commits a crime

cybercrime (SY-bur-krime)—a crime that involves the Internet, a computer system, or computer technology

data (DA-tuh)—information or facts

device (di-VISSE)—a piece of equipment that does a particular job

digital (DI-juh-tul)—involving a computer or other electronics

evidence (EHV-uh-duhns)—information, items, and facts that help prove something is true or false; criminal evidence can be used in court cases

guilty (GIL-tee)—found to be responsible for a crime

hacker (HAK-uhr)—a person who looks for ways to break into computer systems

hard drive (HARD DRIVE)—a device for storing computer data

phish (FISH)—to pretend to be a trusted person or from a trusted company to trick victims and commit a cybercrime

pirate (PYE-rit)—a person who uses or copies the work of another without permission

program (PROH-gram)—a series of step-by-step instructions that tells a computer what to do

scene (SEEN)—the place of an event or action

software (SAWFT-wair)—programs that tell a computer what to do

spyware (SPY-wair)—software that is installed secretly and gathers information about a computer user's Internet use and personal data

suspect (SUHS-pekt)—someone thought to be responsible for a crime

track (TRAK)—to observe or watch the path of something

virus (VY-ruhs)—a hidden computer program that copies itself and harms computers

READ MORE

Hanson, Anders. *Detective's Tools.* More Professional Tools. Minneapolis: ABDO Pub. Company, 2014.

Kamar, Haq. *What Is Cybersecurity?* Let's Find Out! Computer Science. Britannica Educational Pub., 2017.

Orr, Tamra. *Crime Scene Investigator.* Cool STEAM Careers. Ann Arbor, Mich.: Cherry Lake Pub., 2016.

INTERNET SITES

Use FactHound to find Internet sites related to this book.

Visit *www.facthound.com*

Just type in **9781543529906** and go.

Check out projects, games and lots more at
www.capstonekids.com

CRITICAL THINKING QUESTIONS

1. What are some ways police protect and record digital evidence they find?

2. Sometimes police return computers to suspects. How can this help them solve crimes?

3. What can police look for on suspects' computers and other digital devices? Use online or other sources to support your answer.

INDEX

Anonymous, 23

court, 26
cyberbullying, 25
cybercrimes, 8, 9

Federal Bureau of Investigation (FBI), 18, 28
fingerprints, 20

hackers, 8, 11, 23, 28
hard drives, 22

labs, 22

phishing, 17
photos, 21
pirates, 14
programs, 11, 17, 22

ransomware, 12

software, 14
spyware, 24

tracking devices, 24

viruses, 4, 6, 11, 12

WannaCry, 13
websites, 24